P9-EEO-051

THE BEGINNING OF THE EARTH

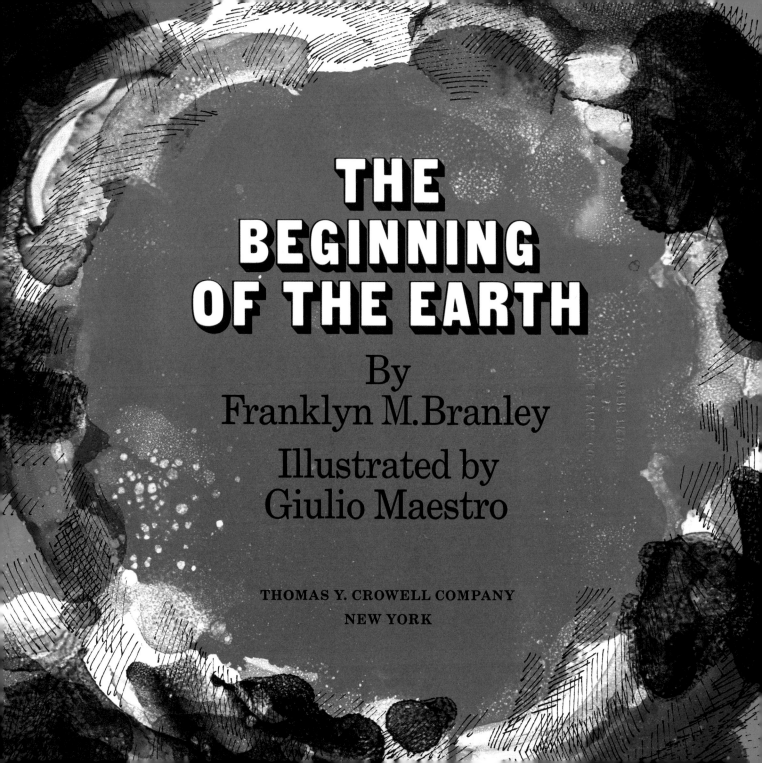

THE BEGINNING OF THE EARTH

By

Franklyn M. Branley

Illustrated by

Giulio Maestro

THOMAS Y. CROWELL COMPANY

NEW YORK

LET'S-READ-AND-FIND-OUT SCIENCE BOOKS

Editors: *DR. ROMA GANS*, Professor Emeritus of Childhood Education, Teachers College, Columbia University

DR. FRANKLYN M. BRANLEY, Chairman and Astronomer of The American Museum–Hayden Planetarium

L.C. Card 79-184979   ISBN 0-690-12987-4   0-690-12988-2 (LB)

1   2   3   4   5   6   7   8   9   10

U.S. 1719493

THE BEGINNING OF THE EARTH

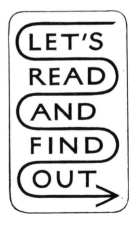

LET'S
READ
AND
FIND
OUT

Where did the earth come from?

That's a question your mother and father have
    wondered about.
So have your grandmothers and your grand-
    fathers.
Maybe you have, too.
It's a question people have wondered about for
    thousands of years.

We don't know where the earth came from.
We don't know how the earth was formed.
But we have ideas about such things.

We know the earth is a planet.

We know it is not the only planet in space.

It is just one member of a family of planets.

We call this family the solar system.

The sun is the center of the solar system.

There are nine planets that go around the sun.

This story of the beginning of the earth is also a story about the beginning of the sun and the other planets.

That's because people believe that the sun and all the planets were formed from the same material and in nearly the same way.

Pluto

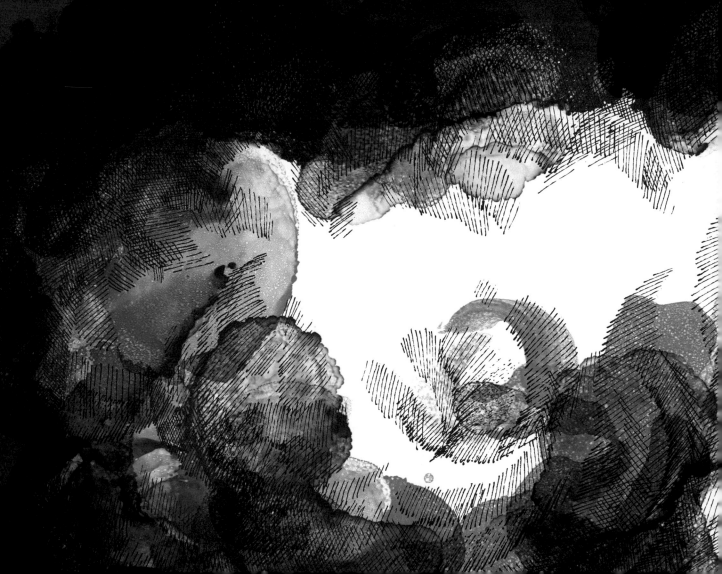

Long, long ago, longer than anyone can under-
stand—maybe ten billion years ago—there was
no sun, and there were no planets.
There was only a great big cloud of dust and gases.

4

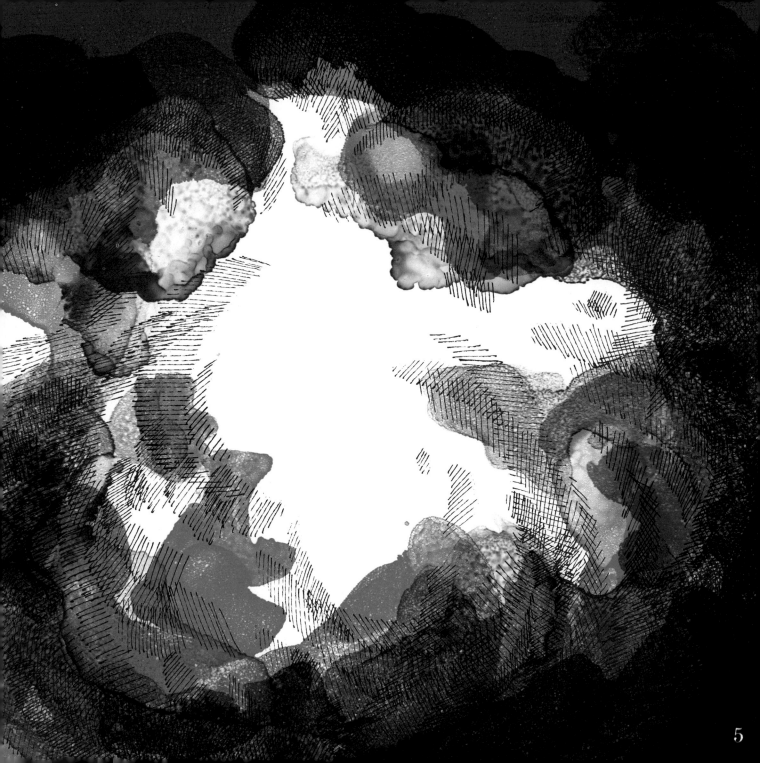

5

Slowly, over millions and millions of years, some of the dust and gases packed together. The cloud began to be lumpy.

The dust and gases packed tighter and tighter. The
lumps became smaller.
The tighter and smaller they got, the hotter they
got.

8

After a long while some of the very hot gases had
    formed into a great big ball.
This ball of very hot gases became the sun.

Some of the gases packed into smaller balls.
These balls became the planets.

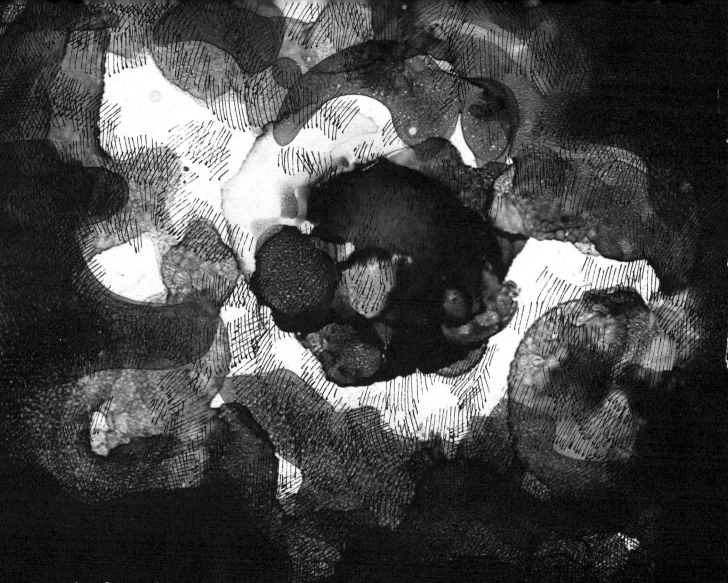

At first the earth was a small clump inside a very
    big gas cloud.
The clump was made of dust and gases tightly
    packed together.

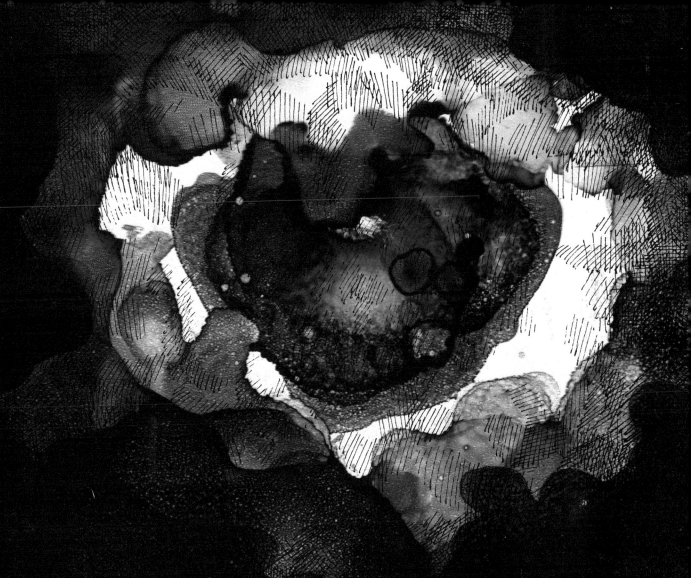

Millions of years went by.
The clump got bigger.
The gases packed together tighter.
The clump got hotter.

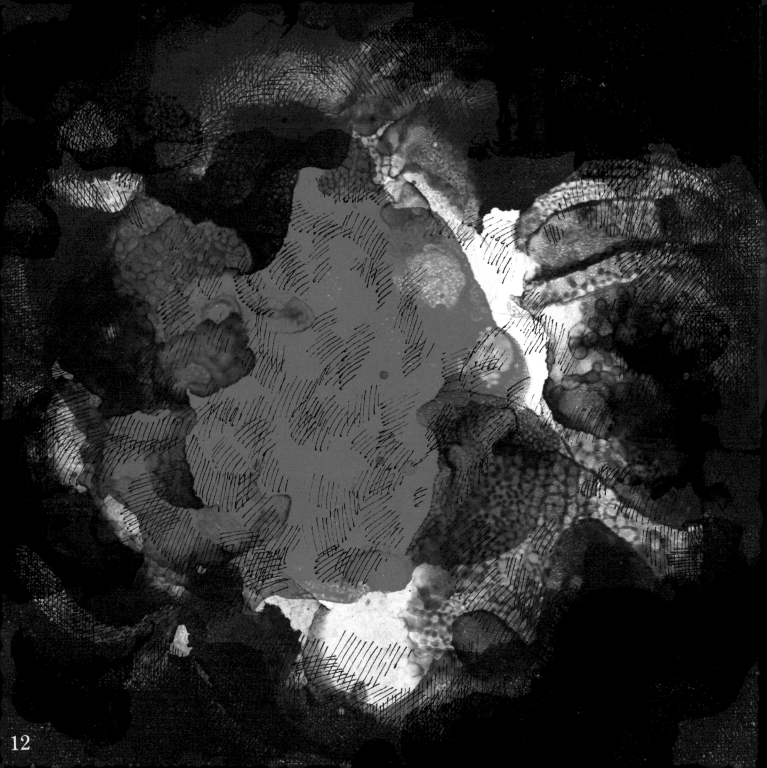

12

More and more gases were added, and the earth-
   clump grew even bigger.
Still it was not nearly as big as the ball of gases
   that made the sun.

The gases of the newly formed earth were mostly
   hydrogen.
But there were other gases, too.
There were oxygen and nitrogen, sulfur and carbon,
   and all the other materials earth is made of.

The new earth was hot, just as hot as it could get.

Then it began to cool.

But because it was so hot, this took a long time.

After millions of years most of the gases were still hot, but some had cooled enough for liquids to form.

Oxygen, silicon, aluminum, and other materials joined together to make minerals—the minerals rocks are made of.

But the rocks were not yet solid; they were liquid.

The earth was still so hot that the rocks stayed melted for millions of years.

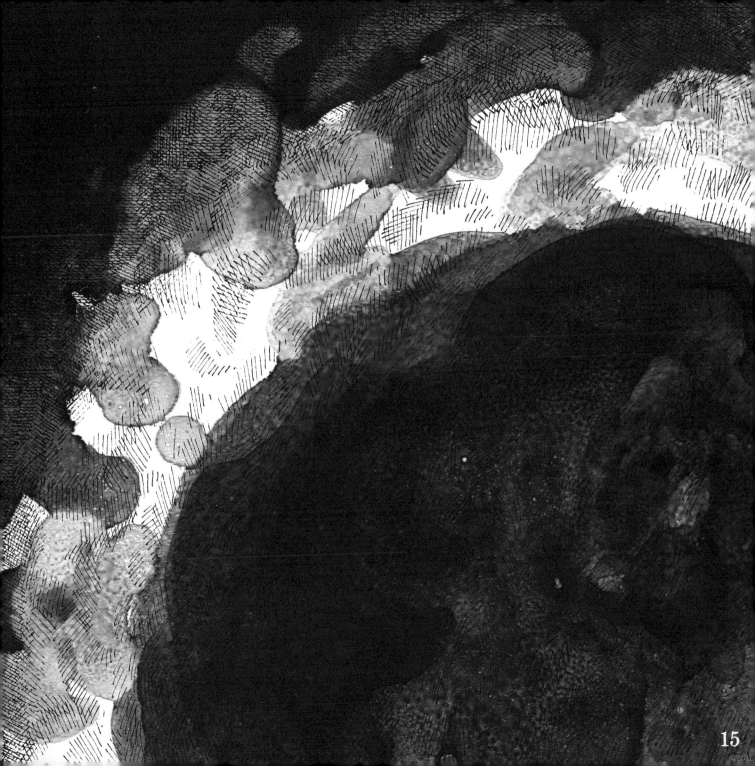
15

Great dark clouds of dust and gases were all around
   the new earth.
High in the clouds hydrogen and oxygen joined to
   make water.
The water fell from the clouds.

But the earth was so hot that the water changed back to hydrogen and oxygen. It changed long before it reached the earth.

17

18

As the years went by, the earth cooled some more.
The rain kept coming for thousands of years. It
came closer and closer to the earth before it
changed back to gases.
At some time, the rain finally reached the earth.
But the earth was still very hot, so hot that the
water changed to steam as soon as it hit the earth.

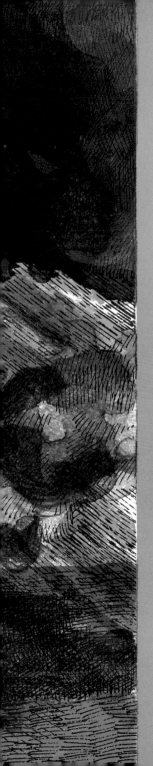

Still the rain came down.

For more thousands of years the earth cooled.

Some of the liquid rock finally became solid.

And some of the rain stayed on the cooling, solid rocks.

The rocks of the earth, and the air and the water of the earth, were formed about five billion years ago.

But the earth did not look then like the earth we
know today.
Five billion years ago most of the earth was still
gases and liquids.
There was liquid rock, and here and there water
that lay on cooling, solid rock.

The solid rock floated on top of the liquid rock.
Slowly the islands of solid rock became larger.
Slowly the islands cooled.
The earth cooled on the outside first.
The inside stayed very hot.
It still is.

23

Dark clouds were still all around the new earth.
Very little light came through the clouds.

For hundreds of years lightning streaked from
cloud to cloud, and from cloud to earth.
The new earth was wrapped in thunder and lightning.
And still the rain came down.

25

For a thousand years and more, hot melted rock broke through the islands of solid, cooler rock.

Red-hot liquid rock spouted out of the tops of mountains, called volcanoes.

Sometimes whole, solid islands were covered by this liquid rock.

When this liquid rock cooled, the islands grew thicker and larger.

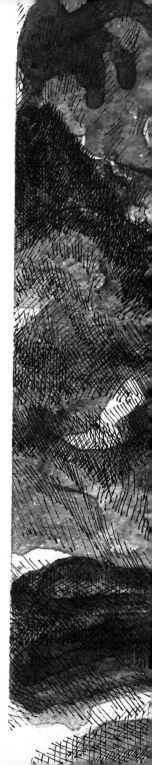

27

Often the islands of earth split as the rock cooled.
Cracks spread through the islands.
Some of the cracks were a hundred miles long, and
    some a thousand miles and more.
Parts of the islands were lifted up.

Other parts sank.
Mountains and valleys were formed.
The sunken areas were basins.
Hot water flowed into them as it rained from the
dark clouds overhead.

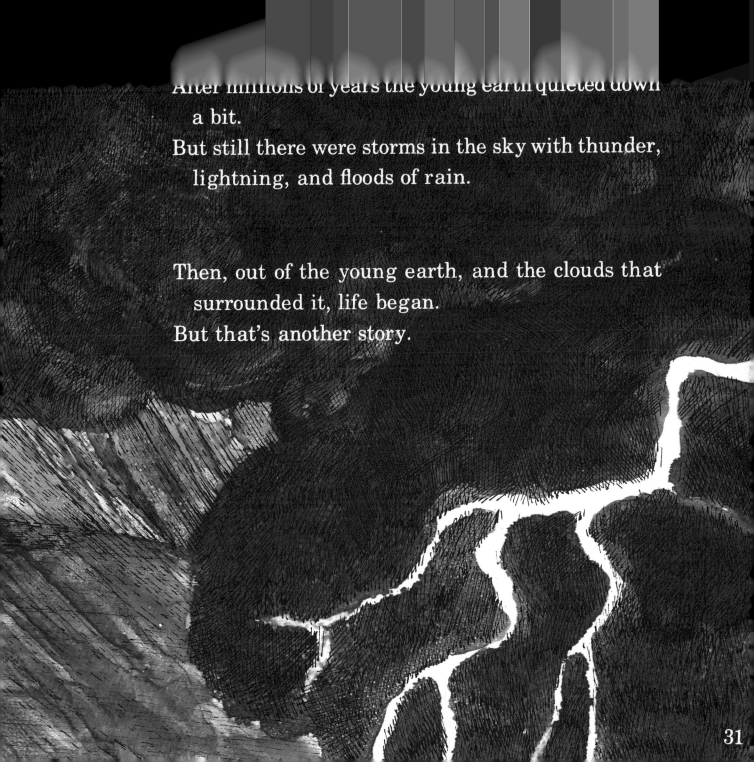

After millions of years the young earth quieted down
a bit.
But still there were storms in the sky with thunder,
lightning, and floods of rain.

Then, out of the young earth, and the clouds that
surrounded it, life began.
But that's another story.

We think the sun is at least five billion years old.
We think the earth is about the same age.
And we think the earth came from the same cloud
   of dust and gases that gave birth to the sun.
So did all the other planets.

But, you ask, where did that cloud of dust and
   gases come from?

That's a good question.
But it is one we cannot answer now.
We must wait until we find out a lot more about this
   earth of ours.
We must also find out about the sun, the moon, the
   stars, and the whole big universe of which our
   planet is only one little part.

ABOUT THE AUTHOR

Franklyn M. Branley, Chairman and Astronomer of The American Museum-Hayden Planetarium, is well known as the author of many books about astronomy and other sciences for young people of all ages. He is also coeditor of the Let's Read-and-Find-Out Science Books.

Dr. Branley holds degrees from New York University, Columbia University, and the State University of New York College at New Paltz. He and his wife live in Woodcliff Lake, New Jersey.

ABOUT THE ILLUSTRATOR

Giulio Maestro was born in New York City and studied at the Cooper Union Art School and Pratt Graphics Center. Aside from writing and illustrating picture books, he is well known for his beautiful hand lettering and book-jacket design. He enjoys etching and painting in his free time.

"I find illustrating THE BEGINNING OF THE EARTH an interesting project," he says, "because although this book is intended for young children, the subject, with its quality of the unknown and the mysterious, holds a fascination for all adults as well."